A monarch butterfly searches for a milkweed plant.

The butterfly lands on a leaf. She gently presses a tiny egg on to it. The egg is the beginning of another . . .

MONARCH BUTTERFLY
New and Updated

BY GAIL GIBBONS

HOLIDAY HOUSE
NEW YORK

For Kate Briggs

Special thanks to Christine Johnson, Curatorial Associate,
Division of Invertebrate Zoology, American Museum of Natural History

Copyright © 1989, 2021 by Gail Gibbons
HOLIDAY HOUSE is registered in the
U.S. Patent and Trademark Office.
Printed and bound in September 2020 at Leo Paper, Heshan, China.
Second Edition

The Library of Congress has cataloged the previous edition as follows:
Library of Congress Cataloging-in-Publication Data
Gibbons, Gail.
Monarch butterfly / written and illustrated by Gail Gibbons. —
1st ed.
p. cm.
Summary: Describes the life cycle, body parts, and behavior of the
monarch butterfly. Includes instructions on how to raise a monarch.
ISBN 978-0-8234-0773-X
1. Monarch butterfly — Juvenile literature — [1. Monarch
butterfly. 2. Butterflies.] I. Title.
QL561.D3G53 1989
595.78'9—dc19 89-1880 CIP AC
ISBN: 978-0-8234-4831-9 (hardcover)
ISBN: 978-0-8234-0909-9 (paperback)

EGG

It's summertime in North America. A breeze stirs the stem of the milkweed plant. The monarch egg is white and shiny. It is the size of a small dot and sticks to the leaf.

When the butterfly lays her egg, she makes it sticky like glue. Wind and rain cannot make the egg come loose.

CATERPILLAR or LARVA

In a few days the egg hatches. Out crawls a small caterpillar, also called a larva. First the caterpillar eats its eggshell. Then it begins to eat the milkweed leaf. The egg of a monarch is almost always laid on a milkweed plant, because a milkweed leaf will be its food.

MOLTING

The caterpillar eats and grows and begins to change. When the caterpillar gets too big for its old skin, it breaks out of it and shows the new skin underneath. This is called molting.

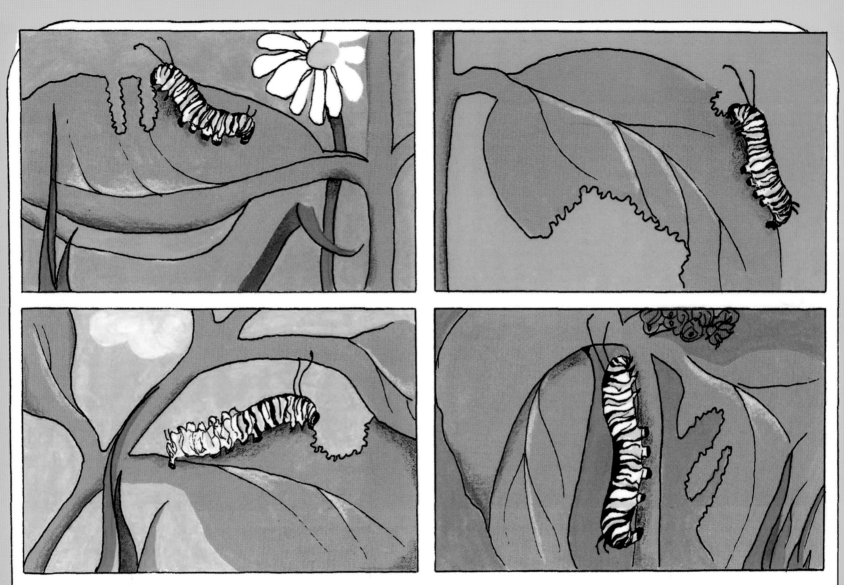

For two weeks the caterpillar eats and eats the milkweed leaves. As it grows bigger and bigger, it will molt about five times. Finally it is a full-grown monarch caterpillar, about two inches long.

When the caterpillar is full-grown, it stops eating and
something wonderful begins to happen. The caterpillar
creeps to the stem of a leaf and drops down headfirst.
The caterpillar's bright colors become greenish.

CHRYSALIS
(KRISS-uh-liss)
or
PUPA
(PEW-pa)

Next, the caterpillar's skin splits open at the back of the head. It continues splitting until it falls off. This new form is called a chrysalis or pupa. The chrysalis is like a blanket that is wrapped around the body growing inside.

11

At first, the chrysalis is long and soft. Then it shrinks and hardens, and becomes light green decorated with gold dots. Inside, the monarch butterfly begins to grow.

About two weeks later, or just before the monarch
butterfly comes out of the chrysalis . . .

13

. . . the chrysalis wiggles. Then it splits open. The butterfly begins to pull itself out. Its head and legs appear first, and then the abdomen and wings slide out.

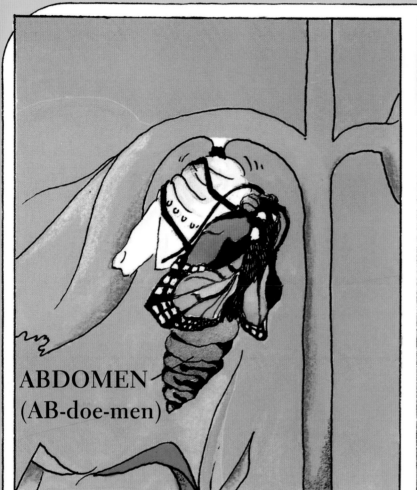

ABDOMEN
(AB-doe-men)

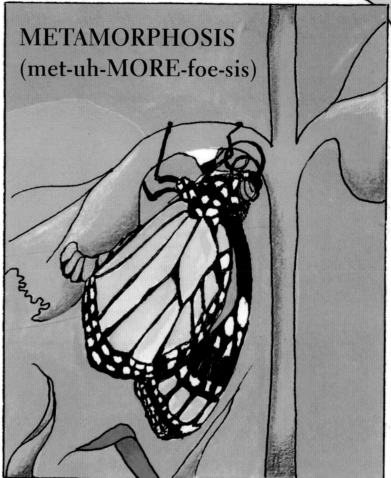

METAMORPHOSIS
(met-uh-MORE-foe-sis)

At first, the wings are crumpled up and stuck together and the butterfly's abdomen is big. The abdomen becomes smaller.

The butterfly sits quietly for a few hours, waiting for its wings to dry and harden. At last they begin to move slowly, and then beat faster and faster.

The butterfly flutters up to the sky. Its colors warn birds and animals that it tastes bad and can make them sick if eaten. Most monarchs are left alone.

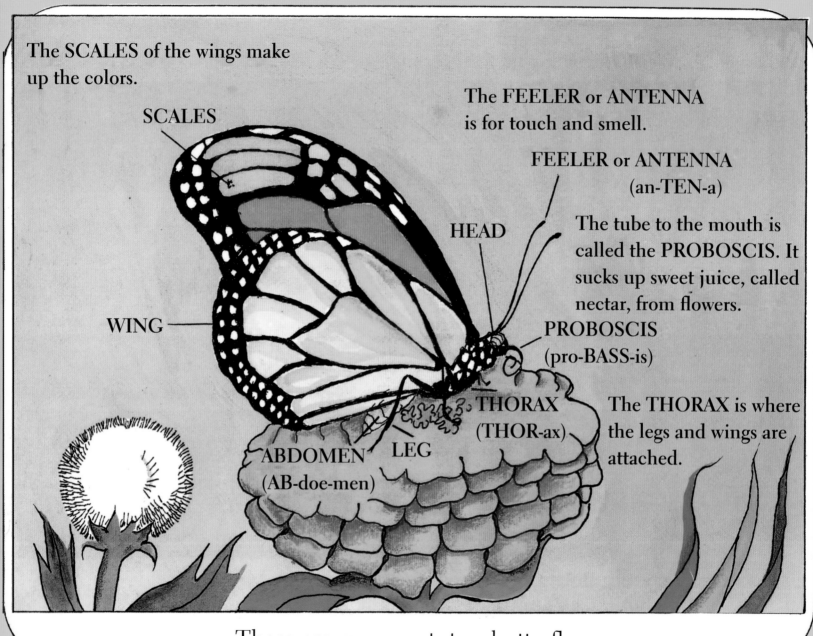

The SCALES of the wings make up the colors.

SCALES

The FEELER or ANTENNA is for touch and smell.

FEELER or ANTENNA (an-TEN-a)

HEAD

The tube to the mouth is called the PROBOSCIS. It sucks up sweet juice, called nectar, from flowers.

WING

PROBOSCIS (pro-BASS-is)

THORAX (THOR-ax)

The THORAX is where the legs and wings are attached.

ABDOMEN (AB-doe-men)

LEG

There are many parts to a butterfly.

The monarch butterfly only flies during the day.
When it rains, the butterfly stays dry, hidden
under leaves.

The monarch butterflies that hatch in the spring
and early summer only live for a few weeks.

The butterflies that hatch in midsummer will take a long trip to a warmer place because they need warm weather to stay alive. This trip is called migration.

The monarch will fly to where its ancestors have always gone . . . sometimes to the very same tree!

Other monarchs keep appearing, making a cloud of
orange in the sky. At night they rest in trees.

Sometimes they fly up to 12 miles an hour and almost 100 miles in one day. There could be over 1,000 butterflies traveling together.

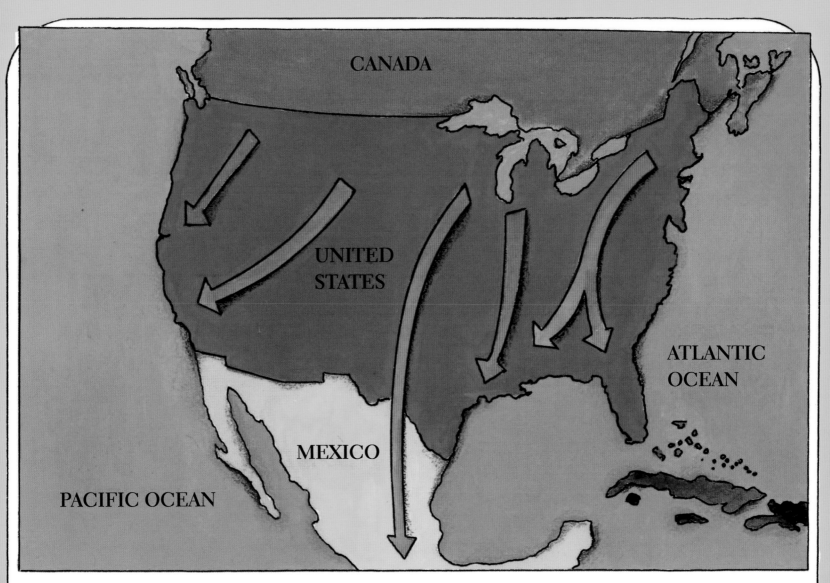

They fly to places such as Florida, Southern California, and Mexico. Some butterflies migrate 4,000 miles! They will stay south throughout the winter.

Some towns and cities are proud to have the butterflies visit them. They have festivals to celebrate their arrival.

Children dress up for parades in butterfly costumes.
Sometimes there's a band, and visitors come from
all around.

Monarchs can cluster together, thousands of them clinging to one tree. A butterfly tree!

In the spring these butterflies will migrate north
again to the fields of milkweed plants.

HOW TO RAISE A MONARCH BUTTERFLY

HOW TO MAKE A HOME FOR YOUR MONARCH CATERPILLAR

Find a big, clean glass jar with a metal lid. Have an adult help you pound several holes in the lid with a hammer and nail, so air can get inside the jar.

HOW TO FIND YOUR MONARCH CATERPILLAR

Late July and August is the best time to find a monarch caterpillar. Go to a field where milkweed plants grow. Look underneath the milkweed leaves. When you find a monarch caterpillar, pick it up gently.

HOW TO CARE FOR YOUR MONARCH CATERPILLAR

Pick four or five leaves off the milkweed plant and drop them into the jar for the caterpillar to eat. Then, carefully put the caterpillar into the jar and put the lid on. Keep the jar out of the sun, where it might get too hot. Each day have someone watch the caterpillar while you clean its home. Replace the old milkweed leaves with new ones. Then put the caterpillar back inside the jar.

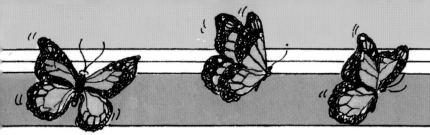

YOUR CATERPILLAR WILL CHANGE INTO A CHRYSALIS

When the caterpillar is full-grown, it will hang upside down from the lid of the jar, shed its skin, and form its chrysalis. Don't touch the chrysalis.

THE CHRYSALIS WILL CHANGE INTO YOUR MONARCH BUTTERFLY

In about two weeks, you will be able to see through the chrysalis. It is time for the monarch butterfly to come out. When it does, it will need a few hours for its wings to grow and dry.

HOW TO RELEASE YOUR BUTTERFLY OUTSIDE

A monarch butterfly doesn't want to be a pet. Carefully let it climb out of the jar onto your finger. When it is ready to go, it will fly up into the sky. Or you can leave the opened jar outside in a safe place.

31

The butterflies that hatch in midsummer are the ones that migrate. They live eight to nine months.

About a hundred million monarchs migrate each year.

Some monarchs fly as high as 2,000 feet.

A monarch can have a wing spread of 3½ inches.

In Santa Cruz, California, a monarch butterfly flag is hoisted the day the first monarchs arrive. It is flown for six months until the last monarch butterfly leaves for the north.

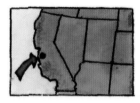

Pacific Grove, California, calls itself Butterfly Town, U.S.A.

The Monarch Project has volunteers who tag thousands of butterflies to track how fast and how far they fly.

In Mexico there are nature reserves where monarch butterflies spend the winter.